Weird and Wonderful Animals

NAKED MOLE RATS

Emma Bassier

DiscoverRoo
An Imprint of Pop!
popbooksonline.com

abdobooks.com

Published by Pop!, a division of ABDO, PO Box 398166, Minneapolis, Minnesota 55439. Copyright © 2020 by POP, LLC. International copyrights reserved in all countries. No part of this book may be reproduced in any form without written permission from the publisher. Pop!™ is a trademark and logo of POP, LLC.

Printed in the United States of America, North Mankato, Minnesota.

102019
012020

THIS BOOK CONTAINS RECYCLED MATERIALS

Cover Photo: Joel Sartore/National Geographic Image Collection/Getty Images
Interior Photos: Joel Sartore/National Geographic Image Collection/Getty Images, 1; Frans Lanting/MINT Images/Science Source, 5; Gregory G. Dimijian/Science Source, 6, 18; Red Line Editorial, 7; H. Schmidbauer/picture alliance/blickwinkel/H/Newscom, 8–9; Joerg Sarbach/AP Images, 11, 30; Shutterstock Images, 12, 13, 14–15, 17, 21, 25, 26–27, 28, 29 (bottom), 31; Steve Gorton/DK Images, 19; iStockphoto, 20; CB2/ZOB/WENN.com/Newscom, 23; Mark Bowler/

NHPA/Photoshot/Newscom, 24; K. Wothe/picture alliance/blickwinkel/K/Newscom, 29 (top); Wade Payne/AP Images, 29 (middle)

Editor: Nick Rebman
Series Designer: Jake Slavik

Library of Congress Control Number: 2019942420

Publisher's Cataloging-in-Publication Data

Names: Bassier, Emma, author.

Title: Naked mole rats / by Emma Bassier

Description: Minneapolis, Minnesota : Pop!, 2020 | Series: Weird and wonderful animals | Includes online resources and index.

Identifiers: ISBN 9781532166075 (lib. bdg.) | ISBN 9781644943373 (pbk.) | ISBN 9781532167393 (ebook)

Subjects: LCSH: Naked mole rat--Juvenile literature. | Rodents--Behavior--Juvenile literature. | Oddities--Juvenile literature. | Burrowing animals --Juvenile literature. | Mammals --Juvenile literature.

Classification: DDC 599.359--dc23

WELCOME TO
DiscoverRoo!

Pop open this book and you'll find QR codes loaded with information, so you can learn even more!

Scan this code* and others like it while you read, or visit the website below to make this book pop!

popbooksonline.com/naked-mole-rats

*Scanning QR codes requires a web-enabled smart device with a QR code reader app and a camera.

TABLE OF
CONTENTS

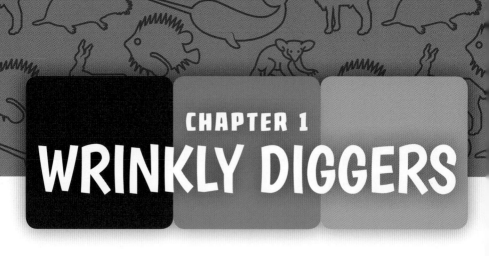

CHAPTER 1
WRINKLY DIGGERS

A pinkish-gray body wiggles down a dark hole. A naked mole rat is digging a tunnel in the ground. It shares the tunnel with other naked mole rats. Most naked mole rats spend lots of time digging.

WATCH A VIDEO HERE!

Naked mole rats look for food while they dig.

Most naked mole rats live in the countries of Ethiopia, Somalia, and Kenya.

Naked mole rats are rodents.

Rodents are a type of **mammal**

with sharp front teeth that never stop

growing. Naked mole rats live in dry

grasslands in East Africa.

DID YOU KNOW? Naked mole rats are more closely related to porcupines than they are to moles or rats.

RANGE MAP

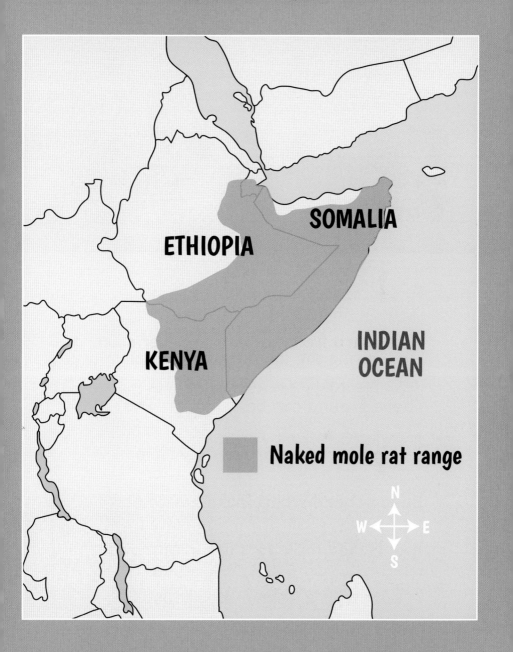

YEMEN

ETHIOPIA

SOMALIA

KENYA

INDIAN OCEAN

Naked mole rat range

N
W — E
S

During the daytime, the temperature above ground can be very hot. The temperature is more comfortable underground where naked mole rats live. Naked mole rats live in burrows. A burrow is a hole in the ground.

The temperature in a naked mole rat's burrow stays at 86 degrees Fahrenheit (30°C).

Naked mole rats' burrows are made up of several rooms connected by tunnels. This underground **habitat** keeps naked mole rats safe from **predators**. It also saves them from getting sunburned.

A naked mole rat weighs up to 2 ounces (57 g). The animal's jaws are very strong. Its body is 3 to 4 inches (8–10 cm) long. However, the tail adds up to 3 inches (8 cm) to a naked mole rat's length.

LEARN MORE HERE!

A naked mole rat uses many muscles when it closes its jaws.

A naked mole rat emerges from its burrow.

A naked mole rat has a short, wide head. Large front teeth stick out of its mouth. The animal chews on hard

objects every day. Constant chewing

keeps the teeth from getting too long.

DID YOU KNOW?

Naked mole rats can move their front teeth independently. They can spread them apart and bring them back together.

A naked mole rat is nearly hairless.

However, the animal has approximately

100 fine hairs on its body. Naked mole

rats have tiny eyes. They do not see well.

A naked mole rat gnaws on a piece of food.

Instead, naked mole rats rely on their

senses of smell and touch.

DID YOU KNOW?

Naked mole rats can make 18 different sounds to communicate.

Underground **habitats** are dark. Naked

mole rats use the fine hairs on their

bodies to feel what is around them.

These hairs help them notice airflow and

ground movements. Naked mole rats

COMPLETE AN
ACTIVITY HERE!

If naked mole rats need to warm up, they huddle together.

also have stretchy skin. It helps them

turn around in tight spaces.

Naked mole rats can get covered in dirt as they dig.

Naked mole rats dig with strong jaws and teeth. Their lips close behind their teeth. This stops dirt from getting into their mouths.

Naked mole rats eat mostly roots.
But they also eat their own poop. The
poop may still have nutrients in it.

DID YOU KNOW?

A naked mole rat's jaws are strong enough to chew through concrete.

Naked mole rats have few

predators underground. From time to

time, snakes may try to eat them. Also,

naked mole rats from other **colonies** may compete with them for space and food.

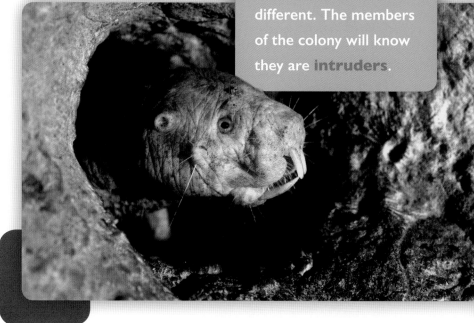

A naked mole rat guards the entrance to its burrow.

CHAPTER 4
COLONY LIFE

A burrow can have 2.5 miles (4.0 km) of tunnels. The tunnels are 1.5 inches (3.8 cm) wide. Each room in the burrow has a purpose. The burrow has rooms

LEARN MORE HERE!

Naked mole rats stay cool underground. Their burrows always stay the same temperature.

for eating, storing food, and pooping.

One room is a nursery for the **pups**.

The average colony of naked mole rats has 70 members.

Each member of the **colony** has a specific job. One female is in charge. She is the queen. She is larger than the other naked mole rats. She is the only female who mates.

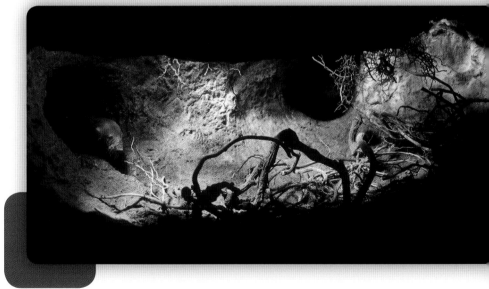

A naked mole rat walks through its burrow.

Most members of the colony are worker. They look for food and dig tunnels. Some members are soldiers. They protect the colony from attacks.

A naked mole rat digs a tunnel using its strong jaws.

To do so, they pile up their bodies and block **predators** from entering the burrow. They also fight with their sharp teeth.

LIFE CYCLE OF A NAKED MOLE RAT

A worker cleans each pup and takes it to the nursery. The queen nurses the pups there for a few weeks.

The queen gives birth to pups. She can have more than 25 at one time.

After a few months, the pups become workers or soldiers.

After one year, pups are fully grown.

Scientists don't know how long naked mole rats live in the wild. But the animals can live up to 30 years in zoos.

MAKING CONNECTIONS

TEXT-TO-SELF

Would you want to hold a naked mole rat?
Why or why not?

TEXT-TO-TEXT

Have you read other books about animals
that live underground? How are those animals
similar to and different from naked mole rats?

TEXT-TO-WORLD

Naked mole rats have certain body parts that
help them live underground. What are some
human body parts that help people live above
ground?

GLOSSARY

colony – a group of animals that live together.

habitat – the area where an animal normally lives.

intruder – an animal that enters another animal's living space by force.

mammal – a type of animal that has hair or fur and feeds milk to its young.

predator – an animal that hunts other animals for food.

pup – a baby naked mole rat.

INDEX

ONLINE RESOURCES

popbooksonline.com

Scan this code* and others like it while you read, or visit the website below to make this book pop!

popbooksonline.com/naked-mole-rats

*Scanning QR codes requires a web-enabled smart device with a QR code reader app and a camera.